DEFYING CONVENTION
WOMEN WHO CHANGED THE RULES

WOMEN
WARRIORS

ELIZABETH SCHMERMUND

Enslow Publishing
101 W. 23rd Street
Suite 240
New York, NY 10011
USA

enslow.com

Published in 2017 by Enslow Publishing, LLC.
101 W. 23rd Street, Suite 240, New York, NY 10011

Library of Congress Cataloging-in-Publication Data

Names: Schmermund, Elizabeth, author.
Title: Women warriors / Elizabeth Schmermund.
Description: New York, NY : Enslow Publishing, 2017 | Series: Defying
  convention: women who changed the rules | Includes bibliographical
  references and index.
Identifiers: LCCN 2016021451 | ISBN 9780766081512 (library bound)
Subjects: LCSH: Women soldiers—History. | Women and the military—History.
Classification: LCC UB416 .S42 2016 | DDC 355.0092/52—dc23
LC record available at https://lccn.loc.gov/2016021451

Printed in Malaysia

To Our Readers: We have done our best to make sure all websites in this book were active and appropriate when we went to press. However, the author and the publisher have no control over and assume no liability for the material available on those websites or on any websites they may link to. Any comments or suggestions can be sent by e-mail to customerservice@enslow.com.

Photo Credits: Cover (top left) DVIDS/Photo by Sgt. Jennifer Schubert; cover (top right) Hulton Archive/Getty Images; cover (bottom left), p. 112 TASS/Getty Images; cover (bottom right) DVIDS; p. 5 Sebastian Meyer/Corbis News/Getty Images; pp. 10, 55, 88 Pictures from History/Bridgeman Images; p. 13 DEA/A. Dagli Orti/ De Agostini Getty Images; p. 17 Attingham Park, Shropshire, UK/National Trust Photographic Library/Bridgeman Images; p. 21 © FineArt/Alamy Stock Photo; p. 25 duncan1890/DigitalVision Vectors/Getty Images; p. 35 Russ Heinl/All Canada Photos/Getty Images; p. 40 Magdalena Paluchowska/Shutterstock.com; p. 44 Private Collection/The Stapleton Collection/Bridgeman Images; p. 49 Print Collector/Hulton Archive/Getty Images; p. 52 DEA/C. Sappa/De Agostini/Getty Images; p. 59 © Steve Davey Photography/Alamy Stock Photo; p. 63 Travel Ink/Gallo Images/Getty Images; p. 66 © David Taylor Photography/Alamy Stock Photo; pp. 70, 100, 106 Library of Congress Prints and Photographs Division; p. 74 Bettmann/Getty Images; p. 77 Beyond My Ken/Wikimedia Commons/File:2015 Fort Tryon Park Margaret Corbin plaque.jpg/GFDL; p. 80 © The Bowes Museum, Barnard Castle, County Durham, UK/Bridgeman Images; pp. 83, 115 © Pictures From History/The Image Works; p. 93 Southern Historical Collection, Wilson Library, The University of North Carolina at Chapel Hill; p. 97 Abraham Lincoln Presidential Library & Museum (ALPLM); p. 110 Private Collection/Archives Charmet/Bridgeman Images; p. 118 U.S. Army photo by Capt. Saska Ball

CONTENTS

War has long been considered the domain of men. While men have traditionally fought on the battlefields, women have always been disproportionately affected by war and, in many instances, have decided to take up arms themselves. Today, in a world where wars seem to be continually waged, women and children account for nearly 80 percent of all conflict casualties. They make up the vast majority of refugees driven out of war-torn nations today and face not only the violence of war but also the threat of sexual abuse and forced marriage. If we state that war is men's domain, we are missing the tragic effects war often has on women.

But that's not the only picture of women in war. Women have courageously fought for their families, their nations, and their causes—whether on the battlefield or off. In fact, some of the most renowned warriors have been women, such as the Egyptian pharaoh Hatshepsut and the famous French heroine Joan of Arc. In order to battle gender stereotypes, many women have disguised themselves as men to fight for their cause, most notably in the American Revolution and the American Civil War. The success some of these women had in disguising themselves means that their courage and daring must be lost to history.

4

War is not only the domain of men. These female guerillas are part of PJAK, a Kurdish separatist group made up of men and women fighting for Kurdish independence in Iran.

Today, women continue to fight, both against gender oppression and to protect themselves, their families, and their nations. The female Kurdish guerrillas in Kurdistan, for example, have taken up arms against the terrorist group the Islamic State (ISIS, or ISIL) in Syria and Iraq in recent years. Their courageousness has been well documented, and they have successfully fought back a further ISIS advance into Kurdistan. These women refuse to be categorized as solely victims of war

Unfortunately, it remains unpopular in the media to represent women as warriors, and their battles remain unknown to many.

A sea change is currently happening in the United States, however, where women in the military are taking on more combat roles. As of December 2015, all combat roles, including driving tanks, leading soldiers into battle, and serving in elite units such as the Navy SEALs, were open to women. It remains to be seen how this will affect American military culture and women's place in it. But, as scholars have been pointing out for many years, women have always been at the front lines of war. In all of America's great wars, nurses, who work in roles traditionally associated with women, have been the first ones on the front line to rescue and treat wounded soldiers.

In a different way, civilian women have always been at the front lines of war, too. They have protected their land from invasion, have sustained their ways of life in the face of war, have born the brunt of war on the civilian population, and have picked up the pieces after war after losing husbands, brothers, and sons. Perhaps a more nuanced view would see war as not occurring only on the battlefield (or, today, in the war room or the drone control room) but as part of a larger process in which women are integral figures—whether as warriors or, more simply, as women in war.

CHAPTER ONE

WOMEN WARRIORS IN THE ANCIENT WORLD

Women had various amounts of power across the ancient world, depending on the time, place, and circumstance into which they were born. In ancient Egypt, women had relative power and were allowed to own property, sign contracts, and initiate divorce proceedings from their husbands. As we will see with Hatshepsut, one of the most powerful women in world history, women could also be pharaohs in special circumstances, usually when acting as regents for their young sons. However, in ancient Mesopotamia, where the great warrior Sammuramat was born, women had more strictly defined roles. They were often viewed as wives and mothers—in relation to the men in their lives—rather than as individuals with legal rights, ambitions, and desires. The same was true in ancient China, where the ancient practice of foot binding shows how women's submission was often painfully enforced.

In the ancient world, war was an integral part of governance. All heads of state, like pharaohs, kings, and chiefs, supported their rule by engaging in warfare, if they hadn't earned their position of power in war. Thus, women rulers were necessarily women warriors. Some women, like Hatshepsut, depicted or disguised themselves as men to establish their power. It is said that Hatshepsut was basically erased from history by the pharaoh who came after her and who, supposedly, was embarrassed at having ruled after a woman. But many women based their powerful positions on their links to male heirs and then held on to their rule for the remainder of their lives. These women often claimed to either be related to famous goddesses or to be the manifestation of divinity, which was another way to legitimate their rule.

Scholars of the ancient world point to the fact that many ancient goddesses were also warriors, which highlights the shared roles of men and women in war, at least before the agricultural revolution around 10,000 BCE. This points to the fact that societal gender norms developed due to the way ancient peoples lived and that women are not naturally less "war-like" or more "nurturing" than men. In fact, some ancient female warriors and leaders were so influential that they, too, were melded with myth and became worshipped as divinities in their own rights. Over time, as cultural norms shifted and gender roles became more circumscribed, these goddesses and historical figures lost the power they held in life when their stories were retold. In some cases, their exploits were ascribed to men. Thus, many influential female warriors in the ancient world have been lost to time.

HATSHEPSUT (CA. 1507–1458 BCE)

Hatshepsut was arguably one of the most powerful and important pharaohs in all of ancient history—and she was a woman. However, her name was largely forgotten because, after her death, Hatshepsut's rivals and enemies erased all traces of her reign, including destroying her carved images across the ancient city of Thebes.

Hatshepsut was born in 1507 BCE, the daughter of Thutmose I and Ahmes. Thutmose was the third pharaoh of the 18th dynasty, in which Egyptian power peaked. She married her half brother, Thutmose II, and became the queen of Egypt at the age of twelve. Upon Thutmose II's early death, Hatshepsut acted as queen regent for her infant stepson but soon took on full leadership of Egypt as pharaoh. Beginning around 1479 BCE, Hatshepsut acted as coruler of Egypt with her young stepson.

Queen Hatshepsut was not just a ruler; she also was a warrior. Hatshepsut's success depended on her tactical excellence and development of an Egyptian navy. Like many great warriors, she also understood the power of peace.

Because it was controversial for a woman to act as the ruler of Egypt, Hatshepsut knew that she had to be careful about the image she projected to her citizens. She claimed that her father had appointed her as pharaoh and ordered artists to depict her in statues and paintings as a man with a pharaonic beard and strong, masculine muscles. She even declared that she was a goddess and not a mere human.

Today, most scholars view Hatshepsut's decision to take over leadership of Egypt as being due to political turmoil during the time, with warring factions attempting to take the throne from her family line. During her twenty-two-year rule as pharaoh, Hatshepsut led military campaigns and fought in Nubia and elsewhere. She also developed a strong navy, recognizing the need for Egyptian sea power.

But, importantly, Hatshepsut was not just a warrior queen; she was a successful ruler who also realized the importance of peace. While at home in Egypt, she focused on building projects and negotiated trading relationships with other powers. In fact, Hatshepsut is known for directing a trading expedition that brought back ivory, gold, incense (including myrrh), and other commodities back to Egypt for the first time from distant lands. Today, her most magnificent building still stands: her memorial temple at

Deir el-Bahri, which is still considered one of the most impressive buildings in the Valley of the Kings.

Hatshepsut died around 1458 BCE, when she was in her mid-forties. After her death, Thutmose III, her stepson and former coruler, erased all evidence of Hatshepsut's reign, perhaps to legitimize his own reign and to deny the fact that a woman had ruled when he had been the rightful heir. However, Egyptologists in the twentieth century gradually began to uncover the power that Hatshepsut had and the importance of her successful reign. Her mummy was found in 2007; today, nearly every museum that features ancient Egyptian artifacts around the world has objects from Hatshepsut's tomb.

SAMMURAMAT (NINTH CENTURY BCE)

We know of the great warrior Sammuramat through the Greek historian Herodotus. According to him, Sammuramat married a courtier of the Assyrian king Shamshi-Adad V while still a young teenager in the ninth century BCE. During their marriage, Sammuramat accompanied her husband on military campaigns, and her bravery is lauded in Assyrian monuments.

Sammuramat married the King of Assyria and took control of the throne at his death. This was highly unusual for the time. Sammuramat also personally led several successful military campaigns.

When her husband died, she became the queen regent until her young son, Adad Nirari III, could rule the kingdom. According to historians, Sammuramat was very well respected in Assyria at this time, which explains why she was able to act as the leader of this empire at a time when women typically did not have much political power. In fact, Sammuramat was the first woman ever to sit on the Assyrian throne.

Sammuramat became such an important historical, and even a legendary, figure that it is difficult to separate fact from fiction. Scholars know that Sammuramat reigned from 811 to 806 BCE and, during this time, fortified the Assyrian Empire and increased stability for her people. Many scholars believe that Sammuramat's power and her success in ruling the Assyrian Empire led many Assyrians to believe that she was divine. Today, we know that Sammuramat personally led military campaigns and brought the Assyrians to victory, returning home to proclaim these victories on monuments and to initiate building projects to show the power of her people. In the city of Ashur, an obelisk was built for Sammuramat, upon which was engraved the following:

> Stele of Sammuramat, queen of Shamshi-Adad, King of the Universe, King of Assyria, Mother of Adad Nirari, King of the Universe, King of Assyria, Daughter-in-Law of Shalmaneser, King of the Four Regions of the World

According to Herodotus, Sammuramat led her troops to defeat the Medes, an ancient

Iranian people, and to annex their land into the Assyrian Empire, and she may have also defeated the Armenians in battle and built the famous ramparts on the Euphrates near the city of Babylon that stood for hundreds, if not thousands, of years and were famous across the ancient world.

But Sammuramat is also known as the likely historical figure that provided the inspiration for the mythical figure of Semiramis. Perhaps due to the power that Sammuramat held, and the esteem in which her people held her, she morphed into a goddess known as Semiramis in Greek literature.

According to Greek myth, Semiramis was a child born from the fish goddess Derceto and her relationship with a handsome, and completely human, man. Derceto left the newborn Semiramis to die, shamed over her relationship with a human. But doves fed Semiramis milk and protected her until a farmer found her and raised her as his own daughter.

Semiramis became known far and wide for her intelligence and her beauty as she grew older and, hearing of her, the governor of Syria visited the farmer and asked to marry his adopted daughter. Semiramis and her new husband, Onnes, moved to the court of the king of Syria, Ninus, and gradually rose up in the ranks of his court.

One day, King Ninus approached Onnes to ask for his advice on how to gain access to a powerful city that was enclosed in fortified walls. Onnes asked his wife because she had proven to give good military advice. Semiramis soon left for the city, disguising herself in clothing that would mask the fact that she was a woman. When she arrived, she noticed that Ninus's military attacked only the most obvious positions along the fortification and did not target the acropolis because it seemed that it would be harder to attack. However, the guards of the acropolis had left their positions to help guards along the other areas of the fortification. Semiramis led some of her soldiers to the acropolis, and they successfully won the battle, gaining access to the city.

King Ninus was so impressed that he wanted Semiramis to become his wife. Distressed that his wife would leave him for the king, Onnes killed himself. Semiramis became queen and, when Ninus passed away, she built a beautiful tomb for him along the Euphrates River. Then, she founded the city of Babylon and went on to rule one of the greatest empires in the history of the world. According to this myth, at the end of her life, Semiramis was either transformed into a dove or was carried away by the doves who had nursed her as a young child.

TOMYRIS (C. FIFTH OR SIXTH CENTURY BCE)

Tomyris was the leader of the Massagetae, a nomadic tribal confederation that lived in central Asia around the Caspian Sea in the ancient world. Not much is known about this tribe, but it flourished during the time of Tomyris's rule around 500 BCE.

Tomyris defended her armies against the Persians and the Achaemenid Empire. Filled with vengeance for the death of her son, Tomyris had Cyrus beheaded, as depicted in this painting, by Peter Paul Rubens.

Around this time, Cyrus the Great, who founded the Achaemenid Empire, was looking to expand his empire from its seat in the modern-day Middle East, and specifically Iran, into central Asia. To do this, Cyrus knew that he had to conquer the Massagetae. At first, he tried to ask for Tomyris's hand in marriage as a way to extend his influence in their territory. But Tomyris rejected his offer. Incensed, Cyrus decided to invade the Massagetae's land.

According to several sources, Tomyris became aware of Cyrus's plans when she received word that he and his troops were constructing a bridge that would lead over a nearby river to Massagetae territory. She approached him first and told him that he could choose where they would battle—either on her land or the land his troops now occupied. At first, Cyrus thought that he would call Tomyris's troops over to where he was located, which would be an advantage in battle. However, an advisor convinced Cyrus that he should attack the Massagetae on Tomyris's own land—they could not risk losing a battle to a woman on his land. This would cause great shame.

So Cyrus devised a plan to surprise Tomyris and to ensure his victory. After a skirmish, Cyrus and the Persian army left behind an abandoned camp for the Massagetae to find. In this camp, Cyrus's men had left jugs of wine. The Massagetae, who were celebrating after this first battle, discovered the camp and began to consume the wine. Once the Massagetae were sufficiently intoxicated, Cyrus's troops attacked the camp, slaughtered Tomyris's men, and took many men prisoners, including Tomyris's son, Spargagises, who was the general of her army. Unfortunately, Spargagises convinced Cyrus to take off the chains that bound him and killed himself before Tomyris could rescue him.

Tomyris was enraged; she wrote to Cyrus and challenged him to another battle. In the following battle, Tomyris led her troops to defeat Cyrus and the Persians decisively. After Cyrus was killed, Tomyris had the Persian leader beheaded and, supposedly, put his head in a wineskin that was full of blood, commenting that she had now satisfied her bloodlust. Herodotus wrote that she spoke these words: "I live and have conquered you in fight, and yet by you am I ruined, for you took my son with guile; but thus I make good my threat, and give you your fill of blood."[1] (This final part, according to the Greek historian Herodotus, may be apocryphal, as he heard it from a second-hand source.)

No one knows what happened to Tomyris after her victory against the leader of one of the largest empires in the world, but the tale of her victory has been passed down for many years.

ZENOBIA (C. THIRD CENTURY)

Zenobia was born in the city-state of Palmyra, modern-day Syria, around 240 CE. At this time, Palmyra was a city-state that was ruled by the Roman Empire. But Zenobia would not be satisfied with remaining a Roman citizen, and she would gather her troops in battle against the Romans, expanding out into Asia Minor and creating the short-lived but important Palmyrene Empire in 270 CE.

Zenobia was known by many names, including her Aramaic name Bat Zabbai. Ancient Latin sources describe Zenobia as an honorable and revered queen, even though she fought against the Romans themselves. One source describes her thus:

> Her face was dark and of a swarthy hue. Her eyes were black and powerful, her spirit divinely great, and her beauty incredible ... Her voice was clear and like that of a man. Her sternness, when necessity demanded, was that of a tyrant; her clemency, when her sense of right called for it, that of a good emperor.[2]

Zenobia was not just a capable ruler, she was also an intellectual. She spoke Aramaic, Greek, and ancient Egyptian, as well as Latin, and

Zenobia led her soldiers into battle with the mighty Romans, creating and ruling the Palmyrene Empire. This intellectual queen was so capable and powerful that even the Romans—her enemies—revered her.

she supposedly hosted literary salons, forming friendships with important literary figures and philosophers like the Greek literary critic Longinus.

In approximately 258, Zenobia married Septimius Odaenathus, the king of Palmyra, and became stepmother to his son, Hairan. In 266, Zenobia and Odaenathus had a son named Wahballat. Just one year later, however, both

Odaenathus and Hairan were assassinated. Because Wahballat was the heir to his father's throne, he became king of Palmyra, although he was only an infant. Thus, Zenobia took over as the queen regent. Soon after, in 269, Zenobia declared independence from Rome, officially marking the beginning of the Palmyrene Empire. The new empress led troops to Egypt, where she was praised for her battle skills. With her prowess and strategic skills, the Palmyrene troops conquered Egypt and Zenobia declared herself queen of Egypt. But Zenobia was still not satisfied. She continued to conquer lands around Palmyra, including areas in modern-day Armenia, Turkey, and Lebanon.

The government of Rome was threatened by Zenobia's ambitions. The new empire captured previously Roman land and interfered with Rome's trade routes. Zenobia held on to this land for several years, and some sources state that the Roman emperor, Aurelian, respected and recognized Zenobia's empire. However, in 272, Aurelian set out on a campaign to recapture lost Roman land. He led his forces into Palmyrene territory and met Zenobia and her forces—seventy thousand strong—at Antioch, now located in modern-day Turkey. The Palmyrene forces lost at Antioch and retreated to Palmyra, where the Romans followed them. Zenobia and her forces were trapped in their own city and, during the attack, Aurelian wrote to a friend, explaining the difficult battle the Romans faced:

> There are Romans who say that I am waging a war against a mere woman, but there is as great an army before me as though I were fighting a man. I cannot tell you what a great store of arrows, spears, and stones is here, what great preparations they have made. There is no section of the wall that is not held by two or three engines of war. Their machines even hurl fire.[3]

Soon, Aurelian wrote to Zenobia to negotiate her surrender. He promised that her life would be spared along with the rights of the Palmyrenes, if they recognized his authority and surrendered the richness of the Palmyrene Empire to Rome. Zenobia, however, disliked that Aurelian did not recognize her authority (he did not refer to her by her title as queen) and refused to submit to him. She wrote, "You demand my surrender as though you were not aware that Cleopatra preferred to die a Queen rather than remain alive, however high her rank.[4]

Soon after writing this response to Aurelian, and fearing that the city would soon be captured, Zenobia escaped with Wahballat on a camel, attempting to reach Persia. Aurelian, however, was tipped off to her flight. He caught up with her and captured both her and her son, bringing them back to Rome triumphantly. Many sources state that Zenobia was paraded into Rome in one of the greatest processions of the ancient world. (A few sources, however, disagree and state that she starved herself on the way to Rome, refusing to bend to Aurelian's will.) After this famous entry into Rome, Aurelian pardoned Zenobia and allowed her to live freely. Eventually, she married a Roman senator and lived in comfort just outside of Rome in Tivoli. Supposedly, she had several daughters and her descendants can be traced until at least the fifth century.

Zenobia's story is rare in that not only did she not die in battle, but that she was granted freedom by those who opposed her and who continued to hold her in esteem. Her life was well documented and, during and after the Renaissance, inspired many artistic works, including operas, plays, and paintings. Zenobia's story is even told by Chaucer in "The Monk's Tale" of *Canterbury Tales*.

BOUDICCA (CA. FIRST CENTURY)

Boudicca lived during the first century CE and was a member of the Iceni tribe, which inhabited parts of eastern Britain during the Iron Age and the early Roman Empire. Boudicca's husband, Prasutgaus, was the ruler of the Iceni

When her husband died, Boudicca was wronged by her his former allies, the Romans. In an attempt to regain their kingdom, Boudicca led her tribe in a revolt against the powerful Romans.

people living around modern-day East Anglia. According to Roman history, Boudicca was tall and had long, blonde hair that fell past her waist. She was of royal blood and was not shy—she would stare icily at those who spoke or acted against her, and she always spoke her mind in her powerful voice.

During this time, soldiers in the Roman Empire invaded and conquered vast swaths of land. Whenever they took over a new territory, however, the Romans were known for allowing previous rulers to stay in power. However, these rulers would have to answer to Rome—and provide both money and soldiers to the powerful city-state, as well. In 43 CE, Roman soldiers conquered the Iceni's land in modern-day East Anglia. The Roman emperor Claudius permitted Prasutgaus to continue as the ruler of his people. However, when he died—according to the Roman historian Tacitus, Prasutgaus died after living a long and prosperous life—the Romans decided not to name an Iceni ruler to the throne, disregarding Prasutgaus's will and taking complete control over the tribe and its territories. Quickly, the Romans began taking over the lands of Iceni nobles and stole money from them. They also committed heinous acts; according to Tacitus, these Roman soldiers flogged, or whipped, Boudicca and raped her daughters.

In response to these attacks on her family and her homeland, Boudicca would lead an armed revolt against Roman governor Gaius Suetonius Paulinus in approximately 60 CE. To do so, she united different tribes, including the Celtic Trinovantes with the Iceni, and led more than one hundred thousand warriors. She was voted as their leader and, before setting out to battle, she let a hare loose in order to divine their fate from the direction the animal took. Then, Boudicca invoked the goddess of victory before preparing for battle.

Boudicca attacked Camulodunum, a settlement where discharged Roman soldiers lived, and then followed the Romans as they evacuated the settlement and fled to the city of Londonium, or modern-day London. There, Boudicca led her army, which burned down many of the structures of Londonium and then continued on to fight and destroy much of Verulamium, modern-day St. Albans.

Eventually, Suetonius, who had fled earlier from Boudicca's advancing troops, ordered his men to fight. They faced Boudicca's troops even though they were heavily outnumbered. According to Tacitus's account, Boudicca and her daughters led the troops from a chariot. As they approached the Roman forces, Boudicca gave a rousing speech about how she was leading her troops to battle not as a queen, but as an ordinary woman who had lost her freedom and had been tortured by the Romans, and whose daughters had been abused. She declared that the gods were on their side, as evidenced by the other battles they had won, and said that she was a woman who was willing to die for her freedom. She told the men that they, too, must decide if they wanted to live a life of slavery or die in pursuit of freedom.

The two sides met at the edge of an open field next to a forest along which ran a Roman road. Unfortunately, while Boudicca's men outnumbered the Romans, her troops were not as experienced as the Romans in open field battle. Due to the way in which the narrow field was bordered by forest, Boudicca was not able to send in all of her troops at the same time. The Romans quickly killed those who were sent into the open field by launching large numbers of heavy javelins. Eventually, Boudicca and her troops attempted to flee but were trapped by wagons that carried their own families. Thousands of Iceni and their fellow tribesmen were killed, and the Romans won a major victory against the British tribes.

Boudicca's fate is unknown. Some Roman authors, such as Tacitus, state that she drank poison after the defeat of her men and was given a royal funeral. Others state that she was killed in battle or that she became sick and died.

Boudicca was lost to history for more than one thousand years. Important medieval historians left her out of written histories of Britain during the Roman era, perhaps due to the fact that, in this period, the idea of a woman warrior was not taken seriously. However, the rediscovery of Roman works during the Renaissance starting in the early fifteenth century revived interest in this important female warrior. She inspired many poems and plays and became even more well-known during the rule of Queen Victoria, who was perceived, in some ways, to be Boudicca's heir and namesake.

The poet Alfred, Lord Tennyson, wrote about this British warrior in "Boadicea," which includes the following lines in Boudicca's own voice: "Me the wife of rich Prasutagus, me the lover of liberty, / Me they seized and me they tortured, me they lash'd and humiliated, / ... Burst the gates, and burn the palaces, break the works of the statuary, / Take the hoary Roman head and shatter it, hold it abominable, / ... Up my Britons, on my chariot, on my chargers, trample them under us."

PINGYANG (CA. 598–623)

Pingyang was born in China in the seventh century, during a time of great political turmoil.

Before the Sui dynasty (589–618 CE), different warring tribes ruled over China for hundreds of years. Emperor Wen reunified China in the late sixth century, but the second emperor, his son, Yang, ruled over this reunified China with an iron fist (some scholars also state that he may have murdered his own father in order to ascend to the throne).

Pingyang was born to Li Yuan, who was a general in Emperor Yang's army. However, tension grew between Li Yuan and Emperor Yang over Li Yuan's ambition. Emperor Yang ordered Pingyang's father to be executed, and he responded by declaring an open rebellion against Emperor Yang. Many others, unhappy with the tyrannical emperor, declared their support for Li Yuan, and China descended into war.

During this time, twenty-year-old Pingyang lived in the capital city with her husband. There were many royalists in the city who sided with Emperor Yang, and Pingyang grew fearful for their safety. She told her husband to escape to her father's troops, reasoning that, as a woman, she would be less threatening to any royalists she might encounter. But after her husband left, Pingyang began to implement another plan: overthrowing Emperor Yang.

During this time, the area around the capital had been suffering from an extreme drought.

Many peasants who lived off the land were starving. In order to gain more support for her cause, Pingyang invited local peasants into her home and fed them. In return, she asked for their military support. Those who agreed to fight with her formed what would soon be called the "Army of the Lady." Pingyang approached other groups and asked them for support as well. Oftentimes, she would need to bribe them with food or a position in the army. Pingyang was immensely successful at this task; soon she had an army of seventy thousand men under her. Pingyang instituted strict rules in her army: the men were not allowed to steal, to loot, or to abuse women. Pingyang also directed the men to provide food for the towns that they liberated from Yang's army. Because of this, support for Pingyang's cause grew; soon, many across China sided with Pingyang and her father.

Pingyang led her troops across China, winning against any of Emperor Yang's troops that were sent her way. Soon, she met up with her husband and father. Together, they destroyed Yang's army and forced him to abdicate his throne. Soon after, Li Yuan became emperor of the China, thus establishing the Tang dynasty and ushering in one of the golden ages of ancient China. During her father's rule, Pingyang was given an important role in the new government.

She became a military marshal in addition to earning the title of "princess," and she also became an advisor to her father.

Unfortunately, Pingyang did not live long after this victory. She died at the age of twenty-three, perhaps during childbirth, just two years after rallying her army in support of her father's rule. According to multiple sources, her father ordered that military music be played at her funeral. One of his advisors objected, saying that military music had never before been played at a woman's funeral. Her father's response: "[T]he princess carried battle drums and assisted me in my quest for the throne. Was there ever such a one as she in antiquity?"[5]

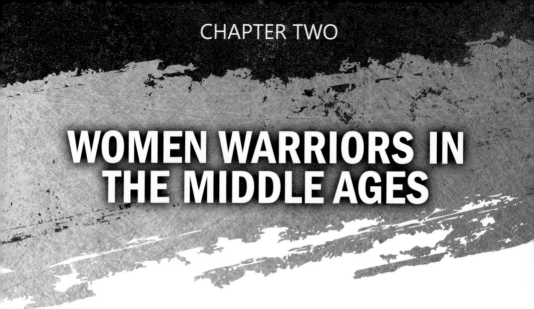

CHAPTER TWO

WOMEN WARRIORS IN THE MIDDLE AGES

Across Europe, the Middle Ages was a period of time that began with larger roles for women in society and ended with more legal restrictions placed on women that would last until the twentieth century. From the Vikings in Scandinavia, to France, to Central Asia, patriarchal societies often placed women's roles in the home, instead of on the battlefield. However, the Middle Ages was a time of great change, too. The most notable exception to the gender roles imposed by society in the Middle Ages, of course, is Joan of Arc, whose name has become synonymous with a fierce and courageous heroine. In fact, many women warriors who came after her were named the "Joan of Arc" of their own nation. It is important to stress the danger that these women faced. Joan of Arc, of course, was burned at the stake, a fate many women who dared to transgress gender rules often faced. (A charge often levied against women who appeared to have too much power or whom powerful men wanted to put in their place was the charge of being a witch. These witch hunts, which often led to the burning death of the accused "witch," occurred throughout Europe largely from the end of the Middle Ages until the eighteenth century.) The charge that sealed Joan of Arc's fate was not taking up arms against the English, in the end, but that she continued to dress as a man while held in prison. The fact that simply wearing traditionally masculine pants and shirts could lead to the execution of one of the greatest warriors in medieval Europe shows what these women were up against.

FREYDÍS EIRÍKSDÓTTIR (CA. TENTH CENTURY)

Many people are unaware that the first Europeans to "discover" North America were not the sailors aboard Christopher Columbus's ships, but rather the Vikings, a group of Norse people from modern-day Scandinavia. Led by the famous Norseman Leif Eríksson, these Vikings traveled to the shores of present-day Canada in the late 900s—nearly five hundred years before Christopher Columbus and his crew. They built longhouses and began to settle

This aerial photograph was taken above L'Anse aux Meadows, a viking setttlement in Newfoundland, Canada. It is similar to the settlement where Freydís Eiríksdóttir displayed brave warrior skills against the local Native Americans.

on the lands around modern-day Newfoundland. Their first encounters with the Native Americans were tense and, eventually, they would cite them as reasons why they did not stay in North America to permanently settle there. The Vikings' first foray into North America is documented in two main accounts, *The Saga of Erik the Red* and *The Grœnlendinga Saga*, both of which tell stories about a brave woman warrior named Freydís Eiríksdóttir.

Freydís Eiríksdóttir was Leif Eríksson's sister. Around 900 CE, she accompanied her husband on an expedition to what the Norse called "Vinland," in northeastern Canada. They began to settle in Vinland and established a trading relationship with the Native Americans who lived there. However, one day, a bull owned by one of the Viking leaders escaped and went on a rampage. The Native Americans, who had never seen such an animal before, grew fearful and took up their weapons to fight.

Freydís was pregnant when Native Americans bearing weapons surrounded her and her fellow Vikings. They attacked, and several of her companions were killed. The Vikings started to flee, fearing for their lives. However, Freydís would not give up so easily. Following after them, she shouted: "Why run you away from such worthless creatures, stout men that ye are, when, as seems to me likely, you might slaughter them like so many cattle? Let me but have a weapon, I think I could fight better than any of you."[1] Then, taking a sword from one of the felled warriors, she began to fight. Due to her prowess and her courage, she saved a great number of her companions and scared their attackers away. (Some accounts state that while Freydís was fighting, she ripped open her tunic and held a sword to her breast, an act that the Native

Americans interpreted as a bad omen and that caused them to flee.)

In another account in *The Saga of Erik the Red*, Freydís is portrayed in a more evil light. According to these tales, Freydís would do anything to ensure her own survival—including killing her fellow Vikings. Supposedly, during one expedition, the Vikings went out on two ships, but one of them began to sink. No one was killed, but a problem soon developed: the Vikings now had only one ship with provisions and food, but now it would have double the passengers. There wouldn't be enough food to go around. Freydís stepped in and proposed a devious solution. The Vikings on the ship that did not sink had to kill all of those who wanted to come aboard in order to guard the food for themselves. The Vikings followed her orders, but they stopped short of killing all of those who had been on board the second ship, stating that they could not kill unarmed women. Freydís was furious, and she decided to, once again, take matters into her own hands—personally cutting off the heads of the women from the second boat.

In another grim story about Freydís, she led an expedition herself due to her status and her reputation for ruthlessness and bravery. Her two brothers and her husband accompanied her on this voyage, but the brothers grew jealous when they saw that Freydís provided the best and biggest ship for her husband rather than for them. They began to argue against Freydís and her husband, thus forming two opposing camps in their group. Freydís could not take any questioning of her decisions and did not want more disloyalty to breed within the expedition she was leading. Thus, upon arriving back in Vinland, she lied and told the Vikings who met the returning ships that her brothers had assaulted her. Once again, the men killed all the Viking men whom Freydís had ordered to be killed, including her own brothers, but could not kill the women. And, once again, Freydís killed the remaining women in the opposing group by herself, threatening anyone who told of these murders with death.

Eventually, the Vikings, including Freydís, left North America to return to Greenland. In addition to fearing that they had outstayed their welcome with the Native American tribes, the Vikings also did not have enough women in their expedition to sustain them in this new land. (If the accounts above are true, this was at least partially due to Freydís's bloodlust.) Little is known about Freydís's life following her return to Greenland. However, in *The Saga of Erik the Red*, when her brother Leif asked Freydís about companions and friends whom she had ordered to be killed, she lied and said that they had decided to stay in Vinland. Eventually, her lie was found out, but Leif could not act against his sister. She lived until a very old age, but as an outcast from Viking society due to her ruthlessness.

It is important to mention that the lives of many famous warrior women were sullied in historical accounts for betraying gender stereotypes of the time. Thus, we cannot know if the more salacious stories about Freydís are indeed true. While the sagas are generally viewed as historically accurate, there is no way of confirming Freydís's role in the murder of her fellow Vikings. We must be content in the only certitude we have: Freydís Eiríksdóttir was an explorer, expedition leader, and warrior who acted against gender stereotypes of the time.

TAMAR OF GEORGIA (1160–1213)

Tamar the Great of Georgia was a queen, a warrior, and one of the most powerful female leaders of the Middle Ages. She was born into the Christian royal family of Georgia, in southeastern Europe. Her family, the Bagrationi family, ruled Georgia for almost its entire history as an independent nation. Tamar's great-grandfather, King David IV the Builder, ruled from 1089 to 1125 and strengthened and stabilized the country. Her grandfather, King Demetrius I, who ruled from 1125 to 1156, was known as a poet and as a fair, if not illustrious, ruler. Tamar's father, King

Unlike many queens mentioned previously, Tamar of Georgia was not a regent. She ruled Georgia in her own right. Tamar was also a brave warrior who personally led her troops into battle.

Giorgi III, ruled from 1156 to 1184. Without a male heir to the throne, King Giorgi realized that his daughter, Tamar, would take over the kingdom. Because Georgia had never before had a female ruler, he announced that he would share the throne with her. From 1178 to 1184, Tamar and her father ruled side by side. Then, upon King Giorgi's death, Tamar became the rightful queen of Georgia.

Tamar was one of the few queens who did not act as a regent or a consort. This means that she was the rightful ruler of the kingdom and that she was not ruling in place of an absent or too young king. In fact, writings dating from the time of Tamar's rule state that she was a *Mep'et'a mep'e*, which means "king of kings."

Unfortunately, there were many critics of Tamar's rule—largely because she was a woman. In order to quell these critics, Tamar cleverly negotiated with powerful players in Georgia to solidify support for her reign and married a prince, Yuri, in order to further legitimize her claim to the throne. Georgian nobles required that Tamar marry Yuri so that Georgia would have a male leader of the military and to provide an heir to the throne. Unfortunately, this union did not last. After two years of marriage, Tamar was displeased by Yuri's behavior, which included verbal abuse and heavy drinking. In 1187,

Tamar began divorce proceedings, accusing Yuri of drinking too much and of other inappropriate behaviors for a king. The nobles granted Tamar's request, dissolving the marriage and allowing her to remarry, which was unusual for the time. Yuri attempted to regain the throne by staging a coup against his ex-wife, but he did not succeed and was exiled to Constantinople.

Several years later, Tamar chose her second husband, David Soslan. With him, Tamar would have two children: George-Lasha, who would become King George IV, and a daughter named Rusudan, who would also become queen of Georgia after her brother's early death. David and Tamar would become very close during their marriage, with David supporting his wife's leading role as ruler of Georgia.

After marrying David, Tamar was able to consolidate her power at home among the important Georgian noble families. Once that was accomplished, Tamar began to look outside of Georgia to expand her territories. She directed her military to conquer tribal land outside of Georgia and incorporated these territories into her kingdom. Thus, Queen Tamar led her country into its golden age.

But Tamar did not just send her troops into battle; in some cases, she led them. According to sources, Tamar addressed her troops before battle, sometimes walking before them barefoot before delivering a rousing and patriotic speech.

Tamar's military campaigns kept both the Georgian noblemen occupied and provided stability for her ever-growing country. Tamar also focused on ruling fairly at home, outlawing the death penalty and ushering in a new cultural age for Georgians, in which Orthodox Christian and Islamic culture were blended in a new cultural identity.

Tamar died in 1213. The location of her tomb has become part of legend, and archaeologists have never located it. Tamar remains an important figure in history: she was immortalized in Georgia's greatest literary epic, *The Knight in the Panther's Skin*, which is considered the masterpiece of Georgian literature. Up until the twentieth century, all Georgian brides offered this epic poem in their dowries. The Eastern Orthodox Church canonized Tamar and gave her her own feast day on May 14. To this day, "Tamar" remains a popular name for women in Georgia, who are namesakes of this important, historical woman.

JOAN OF ARC (1412–1431)

Joan of Arc needs little introduction. She is perhaps the most famous female warrior in the western world. In some ways, Joan of Arc has

Only a young girl, Jeanne d'Arc, otherwise known as Joan of Arc, joined the fight for France in the Hundred Years' War because she believed it was her divine calling.

become a symbol for female martyrdom, righteousness, and, for some, godliness. But Joan of Arc's fame has perhaps caused the true events of her life to become obscured.

Jeanne d'Arc, the French name she was born with, was born around 1412 in the sleepy village of Domrémy, in the northeast of France. Her father was a tenant farmer, which means that he did not own the land on which he farmed; consequently, the d'Arc family was very poor. While Joan did not learn to read or write as a young girl, she was taught Bible lessons and Catholic dogma by her mother, who was a deeply religious woman.

Joan lived during a turbulent time in her nation's history. Starting from 1337, long before Joan's birth, France and England had battled each other over territory in France. Later known as the Hundred Years' War for its long duration, during Joan's life, the English King Henry V took over the thrones of both England and France. This created much greater tension and led to many more battles between the English and the French. In 1422, Henry V's son, Henry VI, took over the throne. During this time, English forces occupied much of northern France, including Joan's hometown of Domrémy.

When she was only thirteen years old, several years after Henry VI's ascension to the French and English throne, Joan claimed that she heard voices. These voices, she said, were messages from God, and they told her to fight for her country (and the rightful king, crown prince Charles of Valois) and to push out the English invaders. At the age of sixteen, Joan left her village in order to claim her loyalty to Prince Charles. In making this decision, she took a vow of chastity and successfully argued in front of her town's court why she should not be married to the man her father had arranged for her to marry. However, when Joan left Domrémy, she continued to face obstacles because she was a woman. The local magistrate in the loyalist town of Vaucouleurs refused to allow her to join the loyalist cause. But this did not dissuade Joan. As she spoke about her divine calling, a group of followers congregated around her, declaring their support for her mission. Eventually, buoyed by these voices, Joan cut her hair short, disguised herself as a man, and began the dangerous eleven-day journey to Chinon, where Prince Charles often stayed at his palace.

Once in Chinon, Joan requested a private meeting with Charles, where she impressed him with her dedication to his campaign and her claims of speaking directly to God. Although Charles's campaign had been failing for quite some time and was near collapse, Joan promised that he would be crowned king of France in the city of Reims, where past kings were traditionally crowned. She asked for an army that she could lead into battle. Almost all of Charles's advisors told the prince that he should not listen to the woman, that she was crazy. But, for some reason, he gave Joan what she requested. In March 1429, Joan rode into battle, an army behind her, dressed in white armor and riding upon a white horse. This was the Battle of Orléans, and Joan would be victorious. During one of the sieges on a fortress Joan and her army were protecting, she was injured by an arrow that struck her between her shoulder and neck, but she continued to lead her troops.

(Scholars are divided as to the role Joan played in this battle. She supposedly said that she led the troops and carried Prince Charles's banner but never killed anyone. However, it is known that Joan's fellow soldiers listened to her, believing her to have divine knowledge, and often took her advice. During the times Joan was in battle, the armies she led always enjoyed incredible successes.)

This victory made Joan famous. Soon, Charles's advisors decided that, if they were to claim that Joan was chosen by God to fight for the righteous ruler, then they would have to prove her moral integrity beyond a doubt. Charles thus ordered an investigation into Joan's background and her religious beliefs in April 1429. The committee "declared her to be of irreproachable life, a good

Christian, possessed of the virtues of humility, honesty and simplicity."[2] Famous religious leaders, such as the archbishop of Embrun and the theologian Jean Gerson, both interpreted the army's victory with Joan as a divine sign and wrote letters of support for her continued role in Prince Charles's campaign.

Throughout the spring and summer of 1429, Joan remained with Charles, leading him across enemy territory and finally witnessing as he was crowned King Charles VII of France in July. She led the army to many victories. That September, Joan advised Charles that they should retake Paris from the English. He agreed, and Joan marched on Paris with her army but, after several days of fighting, they were ordered to withdraw.

In late 1429, a truce with England was reached. Unfortunately, it only lasted for several months. On May 23, 1430, she and her army were fighting forces allied with the English in the town of Margny when she was captured. Joan agreed to surrender and was imprisoned in the Beaurevoir Castle. During this time, the French tried to rescue her unsuccessfully.

In January 1431, almost eight months after her capture, Joan was put on trial by the English. They brought many charges against her, including heresy, witchcraft, and disguising herself as a man.

After her surrender to the British, the courageous soldier was tried for witchcraft and for dressing as a man. She was burned at the stake and later canonized as a saint.

They knew that if they claimed that Joan did not have any divine power but was rather a witch, they could discredit King Charles's claim to the throne. Because of this, the French king did not attempt to negotiate for Joan or to save her.

In May of that year, after being held captive, tortured, and threatened for a year, Joan signed a confession that she was not acting through divine intervention. She defied this account several days later, when guards in her prison discovered that she had once again dressed in men's clothing. This sealed Joan's fate, and a death sentence was handed down based on the now substantiated claim of "cross dressing." (Joan claimed, and others agreed, that she wore men's clothing to deter sexual abuse while in prison.)

On May 30, 1431, Joan was brought into the old marketplace of the city of Rouen and tied to a tall pillar. She requested that two monks hold a crucifix before her, and she tied a small crucifix into her dress. Then she was burned at the stake. But even after her death, her fame would continue to spread. Twenty years after her death, King Charles officially cleared her name of any wrongdoing. In 1920, Pope Benedict XV canonized Joan of Arc as a saint. She has inspired countless works of art, literature, music, and even political and spiritual movements since her death nearly six hundred years ago.

MARGUERITE DE BRESSIEUX (D. 1450)

Marguerite de Bressieux was born a noblewoman in Anjou, France, in the fifteenth century. In 1430, her father, Georges de Bresseiux, the lord of Anjou, defended his castle against rebel troops who were attempting to topple King Charles VII on behalf of Louis de Chalon, the prince of Orange. Chalon and his men targeted Bressieux and his castle. During their attack, Marguerite and her ladies-in-waiting were captured and raped by Chalon's men. After the attack, Marguerite discovered that her parents had been killed. She buried them and then swore vengeance against Chalon and his men. Almost immediately after their burial, Marguerite and her ladies-in-waiting armed themselves and began military training. They learned how to ride in battle and sword fighting, all the while waiting for the chance to battle Chalon and his men.

They didn't have to wait long. When Marguerite heard that royal troops, led by Raoul de Gaucourt, were being assembled to march against Chalon's men, they set out to meet them. Gaucourt saw twelve knights entirely in black, wearing black scarves, approach him and his men. They carried a banner that featured silver tears and heads superimposed over bones. In the middle of the banner was an orange pierced by a

After rebel troups attacked Marguerite de Bressieux's castle, the ruins of which still stand in France, she and her ladies-in-waiting joined King Charles VII's army to exact their revenge.

lance, under which was written *Ainsi tu sera* ("As you too will be").

Marguerite told Gaucourt: "Deign, noble lord, to accord us a place in your ranks. If our arms are weak, our hearts are strong, and bent upon nothing but vengeance. Victims of the most cowardly, the most degrading outrage, we aspire to wash it out in blood."[3]

At first Gaucourt hesitated to allow the women into his army, but, seeing their resolve, he registered them in Charles VII's army. They fought valiantly against Chalon's men, raising their visors to look in the eyes of each of their rapists that they killed. During the battle, Marguerite was mortally injured. She was brought by her fellow soldiers to a local abbey, where she died several hours later. She was buried with full military honors there, and her ladies-in-waiting remained at the abbey, where they stayed for the rest of their lives.

CHAPTER THREE

WOMEN WARRIORS IN THE SIXTEENTH AND SEVENTEENTH CENTURIES

The timeframe from the end of the Middle Ages to the end of the European Industrial Revolution, known as the "Early Modern period" to historians, was a time of imperialism. During these years, colonial powers greatly expanded their influence around the globe. The women warriors in this chapter attempted to negotiate this new power shift while remaining faithful to their nations or tribes. As the queens or chieftains of tribes, women, like Nzinga Mbande, often had more power than women in European society.

NZINGA "ANNA" MBANDE (1583–1663)

Nzinga Mbande was the queen of the Ndongo and Matamba kingdoms in modern-day Angola.

Nzinga Mbande was an African queen during the active years of the Atlantic slave trade.

Born in 1583, Mbande took over leadership of these kingdoms after the early death of her brother, becoming regent in the name of his young son.

This was during the height of the Atlantic slave trade, when colonial powers such as Portugal were consolidating their power over African kingdoms. Portugal focused on modern-day Angola, attempting to colonize it in order, at least partially, to sell Africans into slavery. As queen, Nzinga Mbande would wage war against the Portuguese and force them out.

In 1617, Mbande's brother was king of the Ndongo Kingdom. He sent his sister to negotiate a peace treaty with Portugal in the capital city of Luanda after Portuguese troops had taken over the area and captured many Ndongo people. Mbande was successful at this task, but Portugal did not honor the terms of the agreement and continued to wage war on the people of Ndongo. Shortly thereafter, the king committed suicide and Nzinga Mbande took over the throne.

The first thing that Mbande did was to seek peace with Portugal. She took on a Portuguese name, Donna Anna de Sousa, and converted to Christianity. Unfortunately, this peace treaty, too, did not last. In 1626, war broke out and Mbande was forced to flee from the Portuguese, who entered into her capital. She fled to the neighboring kingdom of Matamba, where she captured the queen, declared herself a ruler of the people of Matamba, and joined her kingdom to it. Then she set up her new capital at Matamba.

The Portuguese now ruled the capital city of Ndongo. In order to fight them and gain back her city, Mbande offered food and shelter to slaves who ran away from the Portuguese and then commissioned them into her army. Mbande also reached out to Dutch colonists in the area and negotiated with them so that they could join their forces to fight against the Portuguese. They agreed, and the armies of the Dutch and of Matamba and Ndongo, led by Mbande, soon attacked Portuguese territory. Mbande led the troops and won a decisive victory in 1644. Then, in 1646, she was defeated by the Portuguese and they captured her sister. One year later, Mbande again led her troops to victory against the Portuguese. This continued for many years, and Mbande was known for personally leading her troops until her late sixties.

Following this loss, Mbande decided to focus on developing Matamba. She continued to develop her kingdom throughout her life until it was an important trading corridor and a powerful nation. Mbande died in 1661 at the age of eighty-one. By this time, the Kingdom of Matamba rivaled the Portuguese colonies in power. Although Mbande had not been able to militarily defeat the Portuguese, she had won in the end. Mbande's new kingdom was never taken over by the Portuguese, and it remained powerful until Angola became its own nation in the late nineteenth century.

GRACE O'MALLEY (1530–1603)

Grace O'Malley was the sixteenth-century chieftain of an Irish tribe, but she is better known for being a formidable pirate who struck fear in the hearts of those she met on the open seas.

Born around 1530, Grace O'Malley (otherwise known as Gráinne Mhaol) was born to the chief of the Ó Máille tribe near Connacht in County Mayo, Ireland. This was a time when Dublin, which is today the capital of the Republic of Ireland, was part of the English Empire. Outside of this big city, the rest of Ireland was controlled by native Irish tribes. Scholars refer to Dublin and its surrounding areas as "a frontier society."[1] The Irish tribes, including the Ó Máille tribe, lived according to their own ancient rules, which involved traditional family and marriage ties, and a system of clientship. O'Malley's father,

Left on her own with a family to support, Grace O'Malley took to pirating on the open seas. The fearless plunderer managed several pirate ships along with hundreds of men.

Owen O'Malley, was the head of his small tribe and, thus, was part of the aristocracy in this Gaelic society. He earned money through farming but also by working as a sea captain, which involved trading with other tribes and nations, charging taxes on those who used the waters he sailed on and presided over, and even plundering and piracy.

Little is known about Grace O'Malley's early years. She was most likely quite well educated and lived a comfortable life in relative wealth. At the age of sixteen, she married the heir to another tribe, the O'Flahertys, named Dónal-an-Chogaidh O'Flaherty. The couple would go on to have two sons and a daughter. But O'Malley's marriage was likely not very happy. Tradition holds that she had to manage her husband's land and other affairs because of his lack of patience and inability to manage his holdings. O'Flaherty was constantly feuding with another tribal family, the Joyces. This feud would lead to his early death in 1564, when he was mortally injured during a fight with members of the Joyce tribe over a land disagreement. Another tradition holds that O'Malley's first battle was to avenge her husband's death. O'Malley led members of her tribe on a raid on Cock's Castle, which was the territory in question between the O'Flahertys and the Joyces. Under her leadership, O'Malley regained control of the castle and it became known as Hen Castle, due to the courageousness of that woman warrior in battle.

According to Gaelic laws at the time, women were not allowed to inherit their husband's lands. However, she was allowed to return to her own family's land and to acquire more land under her own name. Thus, after O'Flaherty's death, she returned to Connacht and made her home on Clare Island. However, O'Malley was in a tricky financial position: she no longer had the finances and land of her husband to depend on. In order to provide for herself and her children, she began to pursue the life her father had lived. With three galleys, or ships, O'Malley began to lead pirating expeditions along the western coast of Ireland, plundering foreign and unprotected ships and leading raids by land and by sea.

In 1567, Grace O'Malley married her second husband, Richard Bourke. He, too, was from an aristocratic family and owned land in Clew Bay, called the Carraigahowley estate. Tradition holds that O'Malley kicked Bourke out of his ancestral home after only a year of marriage, but evidence doesn't hold this as being entirely true. Toward the end of their lives, O'Malley still introduced Bourke as her husband and she continued to live at Carraigahowley.

Many legends surround Grace O'Malley's life. All display her warrior spirit. It is said that she once kidnapped the young son of an earl who had disrespected her. Another legend states that, after having her only child with Bourke aboard one of her galleys, another tribe attacked the ship and O'Malley rose from her maternity bed to fight off the intruders. An English politician who met with O'Malley stated that she had at least three ships and more than two hundred men under her supervision.

In 1578, O'Malley was captured during a raid and was held in Limerick by an English provincial ruler named Lord Grey de Wilton. She was released a year later but was soon targeted for capture by an English captain who sought revenge on her for her piracy. However, he was no match for O'Malley and wrote back home to his superiors that he was lucky to have escaped her attack himself, "so spirited was the defense made by the extraordinary woman."[2]

Meanwhile, Richard Bourke had established ties with the English ruling class and pledged himself to the Crown. In return, Bourke was granted a full title, making him and O'Malley Lord and Lady Bourke. Richard Bourke died of natural causes in 1583, and O'Malley continued to live at Carraigahowley, now as full owner of both her own ships and land and her deceased husband's.

To aid in her domination of the high seas, Grace O'Malley established a series of strongholds along the western seaboard of Ireland, including the Tower at Kildavnet, on Achill Island, Ireland. This tower is believed to have been built by O'Malley's clan a century before her birth, and it still stands today.

However, O'Malley continued to have trouble with the English provincial presidents of Connacht, who were intimidated by the power she held over the area. In 1585, O'Malley's youngest son, Tibbot-na-Long, was captured and held hostage by Sir Richard Bingham. Sir Bingham had been tasked with gaining some control over the land and keeping the different tribes in check, which they resented. Later that year, Bingham ordered his men to capture the land of her other son, Owen O'Malley. During this meeting, Owen was killed. Grace O'Malley vowed vengeance. She led her forces against Bingham for several years. He was tried and acquitted for various crimes against the people of Ireland in 1590, and Grace O'Malley was pardoned by the Crown. However, continued fighting with Bingham led to the destruction of her land and territory by 1592. She was left with nothing, and her son Tibbot was captured once again.

In 1593, O'Malley wrote a letter of appeal to Queen Elizabeth. Fearful for her son's life, she set sail for the English court soon after sending the letter. The letter detailed the crimes Bingham had committed against her, her family, and her tribe, and stated her fear that her son would be unjustly executed before receiving a fair trial.

Bingham heard about O'Malley's plans and tried to convince the queen to refuse to see

O'Malley, but Queen Elizabeth agreed to listen to the Irish chieftain's claims against him. After investigating her claims, Queen Elizabeth ordered that Tibbot be released and that O'Malley receive a pension for the rest of her life. She also ordered Bingham to "protect them to live in peace and enjoy their livelihoods," stating that O'Malley "as long as she lives, [will] continue a dutiful subject."[3] Bingham refused these orders, however, and O'Malley, fearful to return home at the mercy of Bingham, once again asked for the aid of Queen Elizabeth. Her claims were once again investigated and this time, Bingham was captured and imprisoned.

Grace O'Malley died in 1603, the same year that Queen Elizabeth passed away. O'Malley's fame grew even after her death and she has become a national heroine in Ireland and even the personification of the nation itself. She has inspired many works of art, including novels, plays, and music.

THE MAID OF LILLIARD (CA. EARLY 1500S)

Known only as the "Maid of Lilliard," this Scottish warrior was instrumental in the Scots' victory against English forces during the Battle

Lilliard's Stone is a grave marker in Scotland commemorating the Maid of Lilliard's death during the Battle of Ancrum.

of Ancrum Moor in 1545. This battle took part during the so-called Rough Wooing conflict between Scotland and England, where England tried to create an alliance with Scotland and gain some influence over the country to the north.

Maid Lilliard was born in the early 1500s to a family in the town of Maxton, Scotland, which was the site of a massacre carried out by English forces in 1544. Supposedly, her family was killed during this massacre, which spurred Lilliard on to fight against the English in revenge. Now orphaned, Lilliard traveled from Maxton in search of Red Douglas, otherwise known as George Douglas, the 4th earl of Angus, who was a Scottish nobleman and chief who waged war against English forces in Scotland.

Not much is known about Lilliard except that she took up arms during the important Battle of Ancrum Moor with Red Douglas's army against an English army led by Sir Ralph Evers. Evers was notorious in Scotland for committing atrocities during the war, including locking up a Scottish noblewoman and her children in a tower before setting fire to it. His army pillaged the south of Scotland and killed Scottish civilians with impunity. According to some accounts, Lilliard fought valiantly in battle, despite being injured, and ended up killing Evers herself. Even if Lilliard did not kill the brutal military leader, she is credited with Red Douglas's victory over Evers. Following the Scottish victory at the Battle of Ancrum Moor, the English temporarily stopped attacks against Scotland.

Near the site of this battle lies Lilliard's gravestone, with the following inscription:

> *Fair maiden Lilliard lies under this stane,*
> *Little was her stature, but great was her fame,*
> *Upon the English loons she laid many thumps,*
> *And when her legs were smitten off she fought upon her*
> *stumps.*

Today, many people doubt whether or not the inscription is based on what actually happened to Lilliard during the battle, or if it was embellished after her death. However, it is generally accepted that a woman named Lilliard did lead the Scottish troops to victory at this battle and that she died while fighting courageously. Lilliard continues to be a well-known nationalist heroine in Scotland.

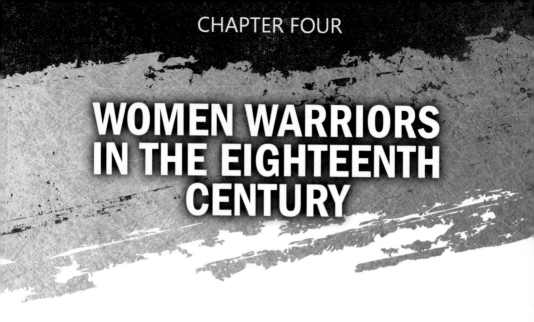

CHAPTER FOUR

WOMEN WARRIORS IN THE EIGHTEENTH CENTURY

Two revolutions that changed the course of global history occurred in the eighteenth century: the American Revolution (1775–1783) and the French Revolution (1789–1799). Women played large roles in both, on and off the battlefield.

In the American Revolution, women acted as spies and disguised themselves as men to fight in battles. While not one single woman signed the Declaration of Independence (women would not even be allowed to vote for another 150 years in the United States), women warriors did play an important role in liberating and forming this new nation. Today, we know of many women who joined the military, some of whom, like Margaret Corbin, enlisted following their husbands, while other women enlisted for financial or patriotic reasons. Often, women who did not follow their husbands

Women, such as Molly Pitcher, took part in the American Revolution, both on and off the battlefield.

into battle were treated more harshly upon their discovery; a woman named Ann Bailey was put in jail for several weeks for joining the war effort to gain a military pension rather than for joining to remain close to a spouse.

Women were also integral to the French Revolution. Before 1789, French women had no legal or political rights and women joined the revolution to vociferously call to revise their own statuses as legal citizens of France. While in the early revolution women's clubs such as the Society of Revolutionary Republican Women gained power and influence, these attempts at including women into the political process of France were eventually crushed. By the end of the revolution, many of these women were either put in jail or forced to flee. However, their wartime agitation would open up the promise of a better society for women in the years to come.

Also during this time, great change was taking place in China, where Chinese citizens actively revolted against the Qing dynasty emperor. One of the greatest Chinese female warriors, Wang Cong'er, would lead the largest revolt during this period and threaten hundreds of years of imperial Chinese rule in a traditionally patriarchal culture.

DEBORAH SAMPSON (1760–1827)

Deborah Sampson was born in Plymton, Massachusetts, on December 17, 1760. Her family was very poor but had a proud lineage: They were related to the original pilgrims who had landed in Plymouth. As a young child, her father was believed to have been lost at sea (later evidence showed he had abandoned his family and started a new life) and her mother, unable to care for her seven children, placed the children in different homes. Deborah was passed to several different families before being placed with

Deacon Benjamin Thomas at the age of ten, where she worked as an indentured servant for his large family.

As the revolution began to take hold in 1776, Deborah dreamed of joining the cause. Because she supported herself by weaving and selling clothes, she was able to create a man's wardrobe to disguise herself to enlist. In 1781, she arrived at West Point, New York, where she was assigned to Captain George Webb's Company of Light Infantry. In the military, she adopted the name Robert Shurtleff.

Soon after her arrival, Sampson was assigned the mission of scouting out a British encampment on Manhattan Island. This was a dangerous but important mission that would provide General George Washington with the information that would help him decide whether or not to attack British forces there. On her way back from this scouting mission, Sampson and her fellow soldiers were attacked by British forces, but they escaped unharmed. Sampson would see many more battles during the Siege of Yorktown and other significant military campaigns.

In 1782, Sampson helped lead thirty soldiers into Eastchester, New York. On the way, they were ambushed by British loyalists. In this battle, Sampson was badly injured. She received a gash from a sword on her forehead and, even worse, a gunshot wound on her upper left thigh. Fearful that a doctor would discover that she was a woman while treating her for this injury, Sampson hid her pain and removed the bullet herself. Her identity was safe.

Soon after this battle, Sampson was ordered to take care of a sick soldier at the house of Abraham Van Tassel. Unbeknownst to her, Van Tassel was a Tory, and he captured Sampson and the soldier she was taking care of, locking them in the attic. When the sick soldier died, Sampson escaped and vowed to take revenge on Van Tassel. She came back with fellow soldiers and captured Van Tassel and the loyalist men he harbored.

However, it wouldn't be a battle that would force Sampson aside. Rather, it was disease. In July 1783, Sampson caught a virus that was spreading around Philadelphia. She developed a high fever and arrived at the hospital unconscious. Unable to protect her identity, the doctor who treated her, Dr. Benjamin Binney, discovered that she was a woman. Upon her recovery, he sent her to General John Paterson with a sealed letter. She guessed that inside the letter the doctor had disclosed her secret—and she was right. However, General Paterson was so impressed by Deborah Sampson that he did not punish her. Rather, he granted her an honorable discharge and sent her home with enough money for the voyage and kind words as to her military service.

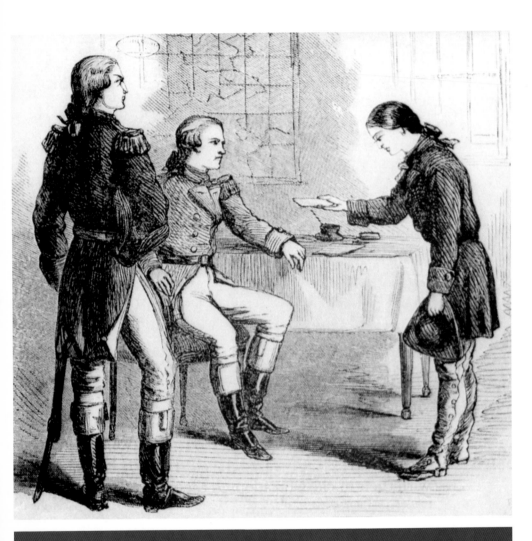

Deborah Sampson disguised herself as a man in order to enlist in the colonial army during the Revolutionary War. This illustration depicts Sampson presenting a letter to General George Washington.

Deborah Sampson returned home to Massachusetts, where she would go on to marry and have three children. After her military service, she successfully petitioned the government for her fair military pension and lectured about her experiences fighting in the war. She died at the age of sixty-six and was buried at her farm.

In 2001, the town of Plympton adopted Deborah Sampson as the official heroine on its flag. She is memorialized in a statue in front of the public library in Sharon, Massachusetts.

MARGARET CORBIN (1751–1800)

Born in the state of Pennsylvania in the years before the Revolutionary War, Margaret Cochran lived through a Native American raid on her village that killed both of her parents. Margaret and her brother had been visiting an uncle at the time of the attack, which saved both of their lives. Becoming an orphan at the age of five shaped the rest of her life. She and her brother continued living with their uncle, who adopted them.

In 1772, at the age of twenty-one, she married a local man named John Corbin. Not long after their marriage, John joined a local militia to fight against the British. But Margaret, who had experienced so much loss at a young age, could not sit around and wait for her husband to come back from battle.

She decided to travel with her husband. She didn't disguise herself or join the battle at first but earned money as a nurse and caretaker for the militiamen.

In November 1776, during the Battle of Fort Washington, Margaret was helping John to load a cannon with artillery. John worked with a partner, too, who fired the cannon after he and Margaret loaded it. Soon, his partner was killed; John began firing the cannon, and Margaret was tasked with loading it herself. But firing the cannon was a dangerous task, as the enemy soldiers could target where the cannon balls were coming from. Soon, John was shot and killed. Instead of fleeing, however, Margaret took over firing the cannon herself. This made her the next target. As British musket balls bombarded her, she managed to aim the cannon with incredible precision. Fellow soldiers in her unit remarked that, though they were losing the battle, Margaret continued to fire the cannon until the very end of the battle, long after every other American cannon was silenced.

Margaret Corbin did not come out of this battle unscathed. She was in critical condition after the battle as a result of being injured by three musket balls and grapeshot across her face and chest. The injury to her left arm was the most serious, and she was unable to use it for the rest of her life. After leaving the hospital, Corbin joined

MARGARET COCHRAN CORBIN
1751 - 1800

DURING THE BRITISH-HESSIAN ATTACK ON FORT
WASHINGTON 16 NOVEMBER 1776 MARGARET
CORBIN WAS WOUNDED WHEN SHE FILLED THE
POST OF HER HUSBAND JOHN WHO WAS KILLED
WHILE LOADING ARTILLERY. THE FIRST WOMAN
TO FIGHT AS A SOLDIER IN THE REVOLUTIONARY
WAR, SHE IS BURIED AT WEST POINT.

CHAMBER OF COMMERCE
WASHINGTON HEIGHTS INWOOD 1982

This plaque, located in Manhattan's Fort Tryon Park, commemorates the courage shown by Margaret Corbin during the Revolutionary War. Corbin took over her husband's post after he was killed.

the "invalid regiment" at West Point, where she continued to help in the war effort. However, she suffered greatly and had difficulty taking care of herself without aid due to her injuries.

In 1779, the Continental Congress granted her a special pension for the rest of her life for her bravery in the war effort. She was the first woman to receive a lifelong pension, although the amount she was given was half of what would be awarded to a man. Her correspondence with military officials documents her requests for more financial and medical aid due to the injuries she suffered in battle.

Margaret Corbin's story made her a famous woman, and she was highly regarded by her contemporaries. Today, three commemorative plaques mark the site near the Battle of Fort Washington where Corbin so bravely fought against the British after the death of her husband. In 1926, her gravesite was rediscovered, and she was reburied with full military honors at West Point.

CLAIRE "ROSE" LACOMBE (1765–UNKNOWN)

Claire Lacombe was born in southwestern France in 1765. As a young woman, she traveled around France as an actress, performing for the aristocracy in their chateaux and country houses. She did not enjoy performing, however, and supposedly grew resentful seeing the extreme wealth of the French upper class. Then, in 1789, the French Revolution broke out. Lacombe decided to quit her acting career to join with the revolutionaries in their fight against the French monarchy, demanding more rights for average citizens.

On August 10, 1792, Lacombe helped to storm the Tuileries Palace with other revolutionaries. She continued to fight even after she received a gunshot through her arm. Because of her strength, she was nicknamed the "Heroine of August Tenth" and received an award for her bravery. During this time, Lacombe became involved with the Cordeliers Club, which was a radical faction of the revolutionaries. There she met another female revolutionary, Pauline Léon, with whom she would found the Society of Revolutionary Republican Women on May 10, 1793. While this club would last for only five months, it was incredibly influential. It was a feminist society that aligned with other radical groups to fight for the revolution; however, it began in response to the deeply engrained sexism in French society. Scholars state that the club was formed, in part, due to the refusal of some revolutionary groups to allow women to use the assembly halls. Together, they demanded that the new French society allow women to

The French Revolution was the cause of Claire Lacombe, who would become known as the "Heroine of August Tenth." Lacombe banded together with other radical women to fight the French monarchy.

vote, to be armed, and to be allowed to enlist in the army. During the meetings, women were allowed and encouraged to take their children with them.

However, as the revolution continued, different groups took over control of the new French government. During the Reign of Terror, the Society of Revolutionary Republican Women fell out of favor and was attacked by other radical groups. In October 30, 1793, the National Convention banned all women's organizations and the society was dissolved. Because she was no longer able to be involved politically, Lacombe returned to her acting career. She was arrested in 1794 for her actions in the society and was released from prison over one year later. No documentation exists for her life after her release from prison.

WANG CONG'ER (1777–1798)

Wang Cong'er was born in 1777 during the Qing dynasty in China. Born in the city of Xianyang, she began her life as a circus performer. But Wang Cong'er would become known as the military leader of the White Lotus sect. Leading the White Lotus, Wang Cong'er would lead a rebellion against the Qing regime.

Born into poverty, Wang Cong'er is variously

said to have performed in the streets of Xianyang and in circuses to earn enough to survive. Her father died when she was a young girl, and her mother gave her permission to beg and perform in the streets in order to bring in money for the family. In fact, it was her life as a performer that helped her master the skills of martial arts. While the details are not entirely known, scholars believe that Wang Cong'er's husband was killed by the order of the emperor. In order to take revenge for his death, Cong'er assembled a large army of peasant men in order to take down the dynasty.

The White Lotus Society was a secret religious society that first developed during the fourteenth century. A political and religious movement that lasted centuries, members of the White Lotus Society often fought against what they viewed as corrupt government through Buddhist-influenced beliefs that included holding men and women in equally high regard. This was revolutionary during this time in China. The White Lotus Society initiated many rebellions against government rule in Chinese history.

In 1794, public dissent over Qing dynasty taxes provoked the White Lotus Society to consider rebelling against the emperor. Wang Cong'er joined the rebellion and organized a large group of men underneath her due to her

中国历史故事连环画　第五十二集

Like many women warriors throughout history, Wang Cong'er went to battle to avenge her husband's death. Wang Cong'er led the White Lotus toward rebellion against the Qing regime.

desire for revenge over her husband's death. Tradition holds that, at the head of the military, Wang Cong'er used both kung fu and acrobatics to fight off her enemies, often performing tricks with a sword in each hand. Cong'er is said to have taught martial arts to women during the rebellion so that they, too, could fight against the Qing dynasty. Although Cong'er's army was made up of peasant men and women and stood against the great warriors of the Qing Empire, they used guerrilla tactics to surprise and disarm the emperor's army. In 1796, the Qing army lost in a devastating defeat to the White Lotus. The fighting went on for several years. According to letters exchanged by Qing officials, Wang Cong'er was the most feared of all the warriors. She was known for having killed two important military commanders with her own hands.

However, soon government officials thought to arm local militias in order to fight and trap White Lotus warriors. In 1798, Qing forces trapped Wang Cong'er and her troops. After a bloody battle, Wang Cong'er's troops were defeated. She and her remaining troops fled to the mountains around Huaishugou. There, Wang jumped to her death after the battle with her banner in hand, preferring to die at her own hands than to be captured by Qing forces.

After her death, many other Chinese women

fought in the name of Wang Cong'er. She became known as a true heroine not just for her bravery in battle and martial arts skills, but for her courageousness, kindness, and generosity. It is said that Wang Cong'er often risked her life for her soldiers, treated their wounds herself, and offered them her horse to ride on, while maintaining the strict discipline required to win against the most powerful army in China at the time.

CHAPTER FIVE

WOMEN WARRIORS IN THE NINETEENTH CENTURY

As in earlier centuries, the nineteenth century was a time when countries that had been colonized by imperial powers fought against their influence. Manikarnika, an Indian queen in the Jhansi State of north India, was a queen regent who took up arms against British officials who attempted to control her state. While in the United States in the middle of the century, Native American tribes were waging their own battles against American settlers and expanding government influence into the Western states.

But another war was being waged in the United States, as well: the US Civil War, which pitted Northerners against Southerners over not only disagreements about slavery, but economic differences. As in the Revolution, American women attempted to join the war effort by disguising themselves as men. In juxtaposing women warriors from different cultures around the same period of time, it is interesting to see how cultural norms dictated how they behaved and, particularly, whether or not they had to hide that they were women. Manikarnika, for example, needed to adopt a son in order to rule the state of Jhansi, but she did not have to hide her gender in order to lead the battle against the British. American women, however, could not join the war effort, except as nurses or, occasionally, spies, except by disguising themselves as men. However, Native American women, like Dahteste and Lozen, were esteemed as competent warriors within their tribes, but they were ignored or misunderstood by American forces that could not understand the role of Native American women in warfare.

MANIKARNIKA, RANI OF JHANSI (1828–1858)

Born Manikarnika in the Hindu holy city of Varanasi in 1828, Rani of Jhansi would become the warrior queen of the Jhansi State in northern India. Born into the priviledge of a Brahmin

The Rani of Jhansi is depicted astride a horse, brandishing a sword and bejeweled. Manikarnika became the leader of a large army assembled to protect their kingdom from the British.

family that had ties with the local government, Rani of Jhansi would enjoy an early life of relative independence. After the death of her mother when she was just four, Manikarnika was taught horsemanship, sword fighting, archery, and war strategy. All of these skills would be put to good use later in her life.

In 1842, Manikarnika married the rajah of Jhansi. *Rajah* means "king," which made Marnikarnika a *rani*, or queen, of Jhansi. The rajah of Jhansi was much older than Marnikarnika, and he died in 1853 when she was just twenty-five. Because they had not had a son, according to tradition there was no heir to the kingdom of Jhansi. (Although, according to Indian tradition, Manikarnika adopted a son who could become ruler one day.) Thus, the British East India Company seized the kingdom, disinheriting Manikarnika. She attempted legal recourse, but the British-ruled courts rejected her claim. In addition to taking away her land, the British East India Company took Manikarnika's jewels and lowered the pension she was allowed as the widow to the former king.

But Manikarnika would not have joined the battle against the British if not for the uprising of her own people. In 1857, an Indian uprising against British rule began and gained popular support. Many people who lived in Jhansi began to support those who fought against British colonization, too, because they were angry that their kingdom had been taken from its rightful rulers.

Then a battle broke out in Jhani. Residents of Jhansi attacked the British soldiers living there, and many of them were killed. Manikarnika was blamed for the slaughter, although it seems that she did not have anything to do with this. However, after this rebellion, she began to gather men and women to join her army to protect her kingdom from the wrath and revenge of the British. Soon, Manikarnika was at the head of fourteen thousand men and women. They expelled any enemy forces from Jhansi and fortified their city.

Soon after, the first British forces arrived in Jhansi to avenge the murder of their fellow officials. From December until April, Manikarnika led her forces valiantly to fight off the British forces. However, in April, they entered into Jhansi and began looting and killing its residents. Trapped, Manikarnika herself led a charge against the soldiers, killing several of them before fleeing with her adopted son and a bodyguard. According to tradition, Manikarnika carried her son over the ramparts of the fortified city and dropped down onto her horse to escape. They fled to a local encampment of rebel soldiers, where they planned the next stage of attack.

In June of that year, Manikarnika led her troops to battle against the 8th King's Royal Irish Hussars. They charged Manikarnika's troops and fought in close battle. According to an eyewitness, Manikarnika fought in close hand-to-hand battle with one of the British hussars while dressed in military uniform. She was thrown off her horse after being wounded by either a sabre or by gunshot. According to one tradition, she knew she was dying and begged her fellow soldiers to burn her body in a cremation ceremony before the British could get to her.

Rani Manikarnika's fame grew after her death, and the British officials who had fought her in her lifetime spoke highly of her braverly, even calling her the "Indian Joan of Arc." Later, she was recognized in India as being a foremother of the fight for independence from British rule. During the lead-up to Indian independence, the Indian National Army established an all-female military regiment, called the Rani of Jhansi Regiment, in honor of her bravery in battle. Still today, the Rani of Jhansi is celebrated across India as a national heroine who fought against British forces for her homeland. She is depicted in many statues across India, and her life is retold in countless movies, songs, and other works of art.

SARAH MALINDA PRITCHARD BLALOCK (1839–1903)

Records show that many women disguised themselves as men and fought during the American Civil War. However, we know of only one woman who fought for both for the Confederacy and the Union: Sarah Malinda Pritchard Blalock.

Known by her nickname "Linda," Pritchard was born in rural North Carolina on March 10, 1839. As a young child, she met William "Keith" Blalock, who attended class with her in a one-room schoolhouse, although he was ten years her senior. They became fast friends. The only problem was that the Blalocks and the Pritchards had been in a feud for many years and across several generations. When they married in 1856, seventeen-year-old Linda faced the displeasure and anger of her family.

Only four years after their marriage, the Civil War broke out. In this area of North Carolina, called the "Tar Heel," villages and even families were divided as to which side they sympathized with. Keith and Linda sided with the Union cause and were concerned that, due to the area in which they lived, Keith would be conscripted into the Confederate army. Together, they came up with a plan: Keith would join a regiment in the Confederate army that would be based out

Disguised in men's clothing, Sarah Malinda Pritchard Blalock served with her husband in the Confederate army as a sixteen-year-old boy named Sam.

of Virginia and from there, because Virginia bordered on the Northern states, he could defect to the Union side. On March 20, 1862, Keith Blalock joined Company F of the 26th North Carolina Regiment—a regiment that would soon be marching north to Virginia.

But Linda did not want to sit at home while her husband fought for the Union. So she decided to take matters into her own hands. She cut her hair short and, wearing her husband's clothes, disguised herself as Sam Blalock. Unbeknownst to her husband, she joined the same regiment he was in, saying that she was Keith's brother. In March 1862, they began marching to Virginia, and Linda was able to meet up with her husband and reveal her plans to him.

One month later, in April, the 26th Regiment was engaged in battle. Keith and Linda were fighting side by side when an intense gunfight broke out. Keith managed to escape, but Linda was shot in the shoulder. She was transported to a medical tent where a surgeon attempted to remove the bullet from her shoulder. In doing so, he discovered that she was a woman. The surgeon quickly reported her to her superiors, and she was discharged from service immediately.

When Keith discovered that his wife had been discharged the night before, he thought of another ingenious plan. He escaped into the woods and found a large patch of poison ivy. Then he stripped and rolled in it. The next morning he woke up with a horrible, blistering rash. He went to the medical tent and, lying, told the doctors that he was suffering from a contagious skin disease. The doctors quickly discharged him, fearing that it would spread around to the other soldiers, and he was free to find his wife. They returned home to North Carolina.

However, the Blalocks would not be left alone in North Carolina. Confederate forces discovered that Keith was at home, uninjured, and told him that he must re-enlist. They escaped before Keith was conscripted against his will and hid with other people who were dodging the draft. Soon, they were able to follow up on their original plans. Both Linda and Keith joined Union forces under Colonel George Kirk and raided Confederate forces in the Appalachian region. They continued to do so for the duration of the Civil War.

Keith did not escape the war unharmed, however. During the later years of the war, Keith was shot in the face and lost his eye. He survived this injury, however. After the Civil War, Keith and Linda moved back to their cabin in North Carolina and started a family. They had five children and spent a happy life with their children and grandchildren until Linda's death in 1903 and Keith's death in 1913.

JENNIE HODGERS (1843–1915)

Among the four hundred documented women who disguised themselves as men to fight in the Civil War, Jennie Hodgers is perhaps one of the most intriguing. After the war, Hodgers continued to live as a man and kept her secret until the end of her life.

It is important to note here that, in a modern context, we would and, indeed, should not state that a person's gender identity is in any way associated with their biological sex. This means that if Hodgers continued to live as a man and self-identified as a man, rather than as a woman, we should respect Hodgers's wishes and use the male pronoun "he" instead of "she." However, because we do not know exactly how Hodgers self-identified or why, we can continue to use the pronoun "she."

Jennie Hodgers was born in Ireland in 1843. Little is known about her life before the war and especially her life in Ireland. However, records show that Hodgers was living in Illinois in 1862 when she enlisted in the 95th Illinois Infantry, which was on the Union side. She used the name Albert Cashier. Her fellow soldiers later recollected that, although she was a bit short, they had no idea that she was born as a woman. She had many friends in her military unit and was considered an excellent soldier.

Woman Soldier in 95th Ill.

ALBERT D. J. CASHIER
OF
COMPANY G, 95TH ILLINOIS REGIMENT

Photographed November, 1864

ALBERT D. J. CASHIER
OF
COMPANY G, 95TH ILLINOIS REGIMENT

Photographed July, 1913

Jennie Hodgers was not the only woman to serve her country disguised as a man, but she was different from most in that she continued to live as a man—Albert Cashier—after the war ended.

Throughout her military career, Jennie Hodgers fought in more than forty battles, including such important ones as the Battle of Nashville and the Red River Campaign. She served for a full three years until her regiment was discharged in 1865 after suffering many deaths.

After the war, Hodgers continued to live as a man. She worked as a farmhand, a church janitor, and even a street lighter. She was so successful in living as a man that she voted—this was before women were legally allowed to vote—and collected her military pension.

In fact, Hodgers lived as a man until she was sixty-seven years old. While crossing the street near her home, she was hit by a car and her leg was broken. She was transported to a local hospital, where the doctors who treated her discovered that she was a woman. However, these doctors decided to keep her secret and sent her to recover at a veterans' home in Quincy, Illinois. She stayed there for three years and, during this time, she began to show signs of dementia. She was then transported to a mental institution, which was the practice at the time, where again her secret was discovered. She was forced to wear a dress at the institution, and news got out that the famous veteran Albert Cashier was actually a woman.

When her former comrades heard this, they couldn't believe it at first. But when they were convinced it was true, they decided that she still deserved to live as she had wanted to live and that she deserved respect for her military service. Thus, she was buried in full uniform during a military funeral service following her passing in 1915. Her gravestone read simply "Albert Cashier." In the 1970s, a second gravestone was added to her grave upon which was engraved the name "Jenny Hodgers."

FRANCES CLALIN CLAYTON (CA. 1830S–UNKNOWN)

Frances Clalin was born into a turbulent time in US history. She was born in the 1830s in Illinois, just thirty years before the US Civil War broke out. Scholars don't know too much about Clalin's life before the Civil War, except that she was married, had three children, and lived with her family on a farm in Minnesota. She would become famous, however, for disguising herself as a man to fight with Union soldiers during the war.

Clalin was not especially rare in any way. During the American Civil War, many women disguised themselves as men so that they could fight in a war they felt very strongly about. Many also joined because they would be guaranteed a salary as a soldier, and they needed the money for themselves or for their families.

In 1861, at the beginning of the Civil War, Frances Clalin took on the name Jack Williams and registered to fight with the Union Army with her husband, Elmer Clayton. Historians agree that Clalin joined a regiment from Missouri and ended up fighting in both cavalry and artillery units. Both

Frances Clalin served alongside her husband as soldier Jack Williams. She proved to be an excellent soldier for the Union Army during the Civil War.

Frances and Elmer fought in the Battle of Fort Donelson in Tennessee. This was an important battle for the Union soldiers because they were victorious and it was a turning point in the war. Clalin was injured during this battle but managed to keep her true identity secret.

In the Battle of Stones River, on December 31, 1862, Elmer was mortally injured fighting alongside his wife. He died next to Frances, but she continued to fight on. Some scholars say that she fought in a total of seventeen battles, was injured three times, and was captured once (before being released). Before having decided to join the war, Clalin had practiced walking and talking "like a man." She was known for being both an excellent fighter and horseback rider. Because of this, she was able to keep her identity hidden for quite a long time.

It is not certain how Clalin's identity was discovered, but many scholars speculate that she was discovered to be a woman after being injured in battle. Others state that she was never discovered, but that she refused the orders of her commander and was, thus, discharged. Whatever the case, she was released and sent home to Minnesota, where she planned to get the money owed to her deceased husband for his military service. On her way back, her train was attacked by Confederate soldiers who took all of her money and her identity card. After returning home to Minnesota, Clalin later traveled to Washington, DC, to petition the government for the money owed to her and her husband. Other veterans set up a fund to help her financially. It was during this time that her story became known, and many newspapers published speculative stories on Frances Clalin's military service. She was able to give an interview and set the record straight: she had, indeed, always kept her identity secret and was proud to say so.

LOZEN (CA. 1840–1890) AND DAHTESTE (CA. 1860–1965)

Lozen and Dahteste were two of the most famous Apache women warriors during the Indian Wars in the late nineteenth century. During this time, many Native American tribes were fighting against western expansion in the United States, which was forcing the Native American population off of their land.

Born in the 1840s, Lozen was the younger sister of a famous Apache warrior named Victorio. From him she learned the skills of a warrior. Not only was she a skilled fighter, but Lozen was also a medicine woman who could heal fellow wounded Apaches. She was said to communicate with higher powers and was able to divine how many enemies there were and where they were hiding just by holding her hands in the air and feeling the number of tingles in her hands.

In the 1870s, Lozen led many women and children to safety while the Apaches retreated across the Rio Grande from the US cavalry. Astride her horse, she made sure that they had safely crossed before telling them that she was returning to the war front to be with her fellow warriors. When her brother Victorio was killed in battle, Lozen decided to join the famous Apache warrior Geronimo.

Born in 1860, Dahteste was a sister of a sub-chief of the Apache tribe. She married a man named Ahnandia and had several children. During the wars, Dahteste first worked as a scout for the US military because she spoke fluent English. However, she soon deserted with her husband to fight with Geronimo's warriors. Dahteste fought alongside Lozen, and they became best friends. Lozen and Dahteste grew to be important warriors for Geronimo, and he trusted them so much that he made them messengers. They would secret information from one group of Apaches to another, a job that required not only stealth, but also intelligence and bravery. Many Apache lives were saved due to their work as messengers.

In 1886, Lozen, Dahteste, and Geronimo were captured by US forces. Dahteste is credited with negotiating for Geronimo, which would eventually lead to his surrender. While imprisoned, Dahteste divorced her husband and remarried another Apache warrior, named Cooni. Both Lozen and Dahteste would be held by US forces for many years. Lozen was transferred to a prison in Alabama, where she died of tuberculosis in the 1890s. Dahteste spent eighteen years in prison and was eventually transferred to Fort Sill, Oklahoma, until she and her husband were released in 1913. Together, they built a home on the Mescalero Apache Reservation, where they lived for the rest of their lives.

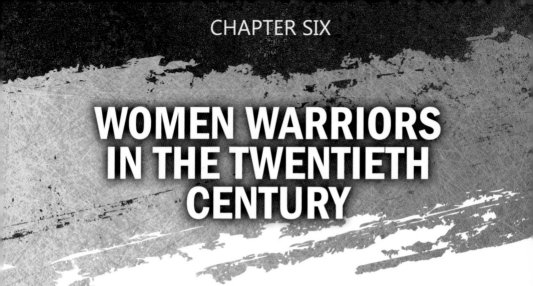

CHAPTER SIX

WOMEN WARRIORS IN THE TWENTIETH CENTURY

The twentieth century brought a lot of changes for women in Europe and America. In 1920, American women earned the right to vote with the passage of the Nineteenth Amendment. Across Europe, women were granted the right to vote from the early part of the century to the mid-century and later, including France (1944), Italy (1946), and Switzerland (1971).

This century also brought two great wars: World War I (1914–1918) and World War II (1940–1945), which both encompassed the increasingly globalized world. Unfortunately, despite great advancements in other political and social realms, women during these wars suffered under gender stereotypes that restricted them to home and caretaking roles. Some women, like Mata Hari, were

By the twentieth century, many women were fighting for equal rights. The suffragette movement in the United States and Europe saw women demonstrating for the right to vote.

not only punished for their roles in the war but also for defying these gender stereotypes. In fact, Mata Hari has become a figurehead of sorts for the "femme fatale," a damaging stereotype of women who use their good looks and power over men to force them to do devious things. Roza Shanina and Kumander Liwayway, two very capable military women, are still spoken about in terms of their good looks instead of their capabilities. While men are often solely judged based on their actions, women are still judged based on appearances and their relationship to men.

MATA HARI (1876–1917)

Mata Hari was a famous dancer and spy who became a symbol of the Western idea of the female seductress and spy. Mata Hari was born Margaretha Geertruida Zelle in the Netherlands in 1876. She was born into a prosperous family, attended university, and married Rudolph Macleod, a captain in the Dutch Royal Army, at the age of nineteen. In the first five years of their marriage, the couple moved to the Dutch East Indies (what is known as Indonesia) to different military bases. During this time, their marriage deteriorated. In distress, Mata Hari delved into learning Indonesian culture, learning the language and joining a local dance troupe. This is where she got the name Mata Hari, which is a Malay term that means "eye of the day" and refers to the sun. She would use this name after separating from Macleod and beginning her life as a professional dancer in Paris around 1905.

Soon, Mata Hari gained international fame for her dancing, due in part to her attractiveness and her willingness to dance almost completely nude. She brought the dances she had learned in Indonesia back to Paris and gained fame in the modern dance movement that swept across Europe at the time and that took inspiration from the East. By 1915, Mata Hari became known as a seductress, and she traveled across Europe often as the companion of wealthy and well-established men.

As Mata Hari grew in fame, she began to attract the attention of the English and French authorities. This was during World War I, when the English and French governments were concerned that their citizens could be acting as spies for the German adversaries. At the beginning of World War I, Mata Hari joined the German intelligence community after being recruited by one of her lovers, who at that time was chief of police in Berlin. She continued to travel during World War I, often passing along intelligence information at her destinations while meeting important military officials and diplomats at her performances.

Then, the French military received a tip that Mata Hari was acting as a spy. She was arrested in 1916 and questioned about her activities. However, she was incredibly clever. During the interrogation, Mata Hari is said to have claimed that she was a spy for the Allied Powers and convinced her interrogators of her loyalty to them. She told them that she could prove that she was, in fact, a spy for the French. They released her, agreeing to send her on a secret mission to test her allegiance to them. For the next year, Mata Hari worked on low-level secret missions for the French government, convincing them that she was on their side, all while transferring important information to the Germans.

Finally, in 1917, the French military intercepted German messages over the radio that stated they had received important information from a spy named H-21. Based on the information they intercepted, French military agents determined that H-21 was, in fact, Mata Hari. On February 13 of that year, French authorities had enough evidence to arrest Mata Hari while in her apartment on the Champs Elysées in Paris. She was held until the end of July, when

International entertainer Mati Hari is said to have used her skills as a temptress and seductress to spy for Germany during World War I.

her trial began for treason and for indirectly causing the deaths of fifty thousand soldiers while passing delicate military information to the Germans. She wrote many letters to her well-connected friends, begging them for their help and declaring her innocence. However, she was found guilty and, on October 15, 1917, Mata Hari was executed by firing squad.

Today, most scholars accept that Mata Hari was indeed a spy, citing as evidence German documents that mention her by name. However, some still believe that Mata Hari accepted money by the Germans but never carried out any espionage activities.

Mata Hari has entered into history as a figure of a dangerous, treacherous, and sexual woman, a femme fatale. Her life as both a dancer and a spy has inspired numerous artistic works, including a 1931 movie starring Greta Garbo as Mata Hari herself.

ROZA SHANINA (1924–1945)

Roza Shanina was born in Yedma, Russia, in 1924 to a peasant family. Roza was incredibly strong-willed even as a young girl. At the age of fourteen, she walked 120 miles (193 kilometers) across forestland in order to enroll in college. Soon after, she joined the Young Communist

Roza Shanina, left, is pictured with two fellow snipers, Alexandra Yekimova and Lidia Vdovina.

League. She was awarded a scholarship to study and graduated college in 1942, at the height of World War II.

Soon, the war would come to where Shanina was teaching kindergarten following her graduation. The town of Arkhangelsk was bombed by German forces that year, and soon after two of her brothers joined the military to fight against them. Shortly after, one of her brothers was killed during the Siege of Leningrad. Shanina was devastated and tried to join the war effort. However, because she was a woman, she was not allowed into battle.

The next year, two more of her brothers were killed in battle. Due to the ferocity of the war, Russia was beginning to allow women to join battle as snipers. In 1943, Shanina was drafted into the war and sent for military training. She graduated from military school with high honors and soon joined a women's sniper unit, called the 184th Rifle Division, as its commander. Her bravery in battle during her first month of service would be awarded by the Order of Glory 3rd Class honor. Her time fighting in this unit was recorded in a diary that she kept that was subsequently published.

In 1944, the Russian government disbanded her unit and the female snipers were sent home. But Shanina refused to stop fighting. Against orders, she joined an infantry unit and participated in several important battles, including the Battle of Vilinus. Due to her bravery while part of the infantry units, she was awarded the Order of Glory 2nd Class, an even higher honor than the award she had previously been given. That same year she was awarded the Medal for Courage—one of the first female snipers to ever win the prestigious award. She gained fame for her bravery—she often requested to be sent to the front lines and, when she was not granted permission, she went anyway—and for her skill as a sniper and high number of confirmed "kills."

In December 1944, she was injured when she was shot through the shoulder by a German sniper. She wrote in her journal that she did not feel much pain and was impatient to return to battle. She did. In early 1945, she participated in the East Prussian Offensive. She received permission to fight in the front lines during this offensive and killed twenty-six enemy soldiers. Over the course of her military career, Shanina would be credited with fifty-nine confirmed "kills" of enemy soldiers.

But, during the East Prussian Offensive, Shanina's unit experienced heavy losses. In one of her journal entries, she admitted that she was braced for death, as her unit had lost seventy-two out of seventy-eight soldiers. Indeed, she was killed on January 27, 1945, while attempting to shield a wounded fellow soldier.

Following the posthumous publication of her diary, Shanina's fame only grew. Monuments have been built for Shanina, and many prizes are awarded in her name. Numerous books have been written about Shanina's life or have been inspired by it.

REMEDIOS GOMEZ-PARAISO (1919–2014)

Known as Kumander Liwayway, Remedios Gomez-Paraiso was a beauty queen who ended up becoming such an accomplished military commander that she became known as the "Joan of Arc of the Philippines."

Born in 1919, Gomez-Paraiso was the daughter of a provincial mayor in the Philippines who gained attention for her good looks. She never considered entering the military until 1942, when

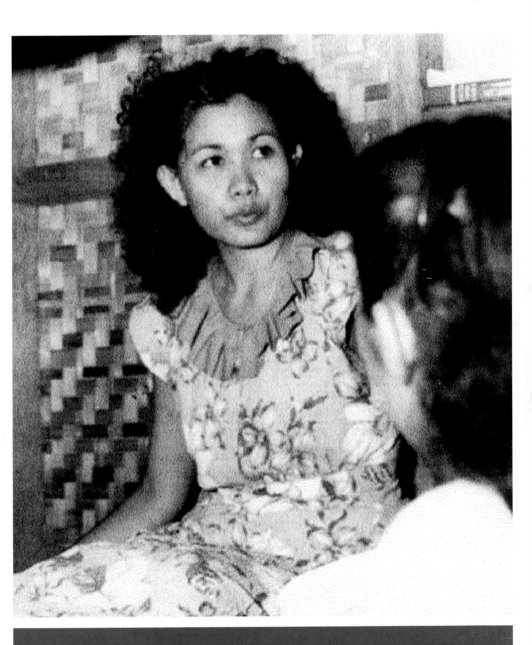

Beauty queen Remedios Gomez-Paraiso joined a band of guerillas to fight against the Japanese during World War II, eventually becoming commander.

Japanese forces invaded the Philippines. Gomez-Paraiso's father attempted to form a resistance group against the invaders but, when he was discovered, he was arrested, tortured, and killed. Gomez-Paraiso and her brother vowed revenge for his death.

Thus, at the age of twenty-two, Gomez-Paraiso left college to join local guerrilla forces fighting against the Japanese. She began as a nurse but, by 1943, she was appointed chief of her military unit. She took on the name "Kumander Liwayway," which means "Commander Dawn," and was known for dressing nicely and wearing lipstick even when in battle. She said that this was important to her, stating, "One of the things I am fighting for ... is the right to be myself."[1]

Gomez-Paraiso was known for her bravery in battle. During the Battle of Kamansi, leaders of the rebel forces decided to retreat, fearful of being vastly outnumbered by the Japanese. But Gomez-Paraiso refused to do so. She stood her ground, commanding one hundred rebels, and fought so courageously that they won although outnumbered by the Japanese. Once, she challenged a fellow commander to a duel when he was acting disrespectfully to her because she was a woman. She also rescued quite a few American pilots who were downed in the forest when their planes were shot down during the war.

Gomez-Paraiso was captured twice during her military career, both times when she was betrayed by fellow rebel soldiers. She narrowly escaped execution both times. During her second imprisonment, her husband was charged with rebellion, found guilty, and executed. She was acquitted, after spending some time in solitary confinement.

Gomez-Paraiso fought until the end of the war in 1945 and continued to play a large role in local politics after her military service, especially advocating for veterans. Gomez-Paraiso was also vocal about the role of Filipino women during the war. She said,

> Filipino women played an important role during the war. Like their male counterparts, they held responsible positions in fighting the enemies. They dedicated their lives to a noble cause not only to drive away the Japanese invaders but [also] to pursue the struggle for genuine freedom, true justice and democracy ... I hope that someday, the role of these unsung heroines will find a place in history."[2]

Remedios Gomez-Paraiso died in 2014 at the age of ninety-five.

Today, women are taking on increasingly important roles in the U.S. military. Their accomplishments and bravery should put to rest the antiquated notion that women don't belong in war.

CONCLUSION

The U.S. military has recently opened up all combat roles for women, which means that they can be on the front lines and join Special Forces such as the SEALs, Rangers, and Green Berets. This has proved to be quite controversial for many Americans, who continue to view women based on traditional stereotypes that state women are "natural nurturers" or "unfit for war."

While we should not justify war indiscriminately and seek to put more women—or men—in harm's way, it is also important to analyze why it is so uncomfortable for people to think about women in war. For thousands of years, women have fought battles due to their own convictions or out of desperation, revenge, or love. These women have proved—over and over again—their courage, their military prowess, and their fierceness.

It's time to start thinking differently about women in war.

CHAPTER NOTES

CHAPTER 1. WOMEN WARRIORS IN THE ANCIENT WORLD

1. Paul Halsall, "Ancient History Sourcebook: Herodotus: Queen Tomyris of the Massagetai and the Defeat of the Persians under Cyrus," Fordham University. http://legacy.fordham.edu/halsall/ancient/tomyris.asp (accessed April 27, 2016).
2. Linda Grant De Pauw, *Battle Cries and Lullabies: Women in War from Prehistory to the Present* (Norman, OK: University of Oklahoma Press, 2000), p. 75.
3. Ibid., p. 76.
4. Ibid.
5. Jason Porath, "Pinyan: The Princess Who Toppled a Dynasty." Rejected Princesses. http://www.rejectedprincesses.com/princesses/ping-yang (accessed April 27, 2016).

CHAPTER 2. WOMEN WARRIORS IN THE MIDDLE AGES

1. Lorraine, "Freydís Eiríksdóttir, Viking Warrior," *Interesting Pretties*. http://interestingpretties.blogspot.com/2012/10/freydis-eiriksdottir-viking-warrior.html (accessed April 27, 2016).
2. Malcolm Graham Allan Vale, *Charles the Seventh*. (Berkeley, CA: University of California Press, 1974), p. 55.

3. H. Savien, "Marguerite de Bressieux." http://
hsavinien.tumblr.com/post/116513781061/mar-
guerite-de-bressieux-was-also-of-anjou-but-she
(accessed April 27, 2016).

CHAPTER 3. WOMEN WARRIORS IN THE SIXTEENTH AND SEVENTEENTH CENTURIES

1. Theresa D. Murray, "Gráinne Mhaol, Pirate
Queen of Connacht: Behind the Legend,"
History Ireland. http://www.historyire-
land.com/early-modern-history-1500-1700/
grainne-mhaol-pirate-queen-of-connacht-be-
hind-the-legend/ (accessed April 27, 2016).
2. Ibid.
3. Ibid.

CHAPTER 6. WOMEN WARRIORS IN THE TWENTIETH CENTURY

1. Tonette Orejas, "Liwayway: Warrior Who Wore
Lipstick in Gun Battles," *Inquirer Central Luzon.*
http://newsinfo.inquirer.net/602758/liway-
way-warrior-who-wore-lipstick-in-gun-battles
(accessed April 27, 2016).
2. Ibid.

apocryphal Of doubtful origin; something that is most likely not true.

Brahmin A higher caste, or social class, in Hinduism consisting of priests, teachers, and scholars.

châteaux French for "castles"; manor houses for a lords.

city-state A city that forms its own independent state, along with its surrounding territory.

commemorative Something that acts as a memorial for someone or something.

embellished Elaborated.

foot binding An ancient tradition in China where high-born women's feet were tied up from an early age and trained not to grow naturally.

galley A low flat ship with sails and oars; chiefly used for war or piracy.

guerrilla A member of, or referring to, unorganized fighting, typically against organized military forces.

imperialism The policy or process of extending one nation's power to other territories, usually by force.

nomadic Referring to nomads, or those who move around from place to place and do not stay in one fixed location.

patriarchal Describing systems of government or society that are controlled by men.

pillage During war or unrest, to steal goods or money out in the open.

raid A sudden attack during war.

regent Someone who rules in place of the appointed monarch or ruler because that ruler is either absent or too young to rule.

sabre A long, curved sword.

sexism Prejudice or discrimination based on one's gender, usually against women.

synonymous Sharing the same meaning.

transgress To go against the rules of a society.

turbulent Chaotic or uncontrolled.

FURTHER READING

BOOKS

Chambers, Anne, and Deidre O'Neill. *Pirate Queen of Ireland: The Adventures of Grace O'Malley*. Cork, Ireland: Collins Press: 2014.

Fraser, Antonia. *The Warrior Queens: The Legends and the Lives of the Women Who Have Led Their Nations in War*. New York, NY: Anchor, 1990.

Mahon, Elizabeth Kerri. *Scandalous Women: The Lives and Loves of History's Most Notorious Women*. New York, NY: TarcherPerigee, 2011.

Mayor, Adrienne. *The Amazons: Lives and Legends of Warrior Women Across the Ancient World*. Princeton, NJ: Princeton University Press, 2016.

McRobbie, Linda Rodriguez. *Princesses Behaving Badly: Real Stories from History Without the Fairy-Tale Endings*. Philadelphia, PA: Quirk Books, 2013.

Women Warriors: Joan of Arc to Malala. Lightning Guides: 2016.

WEBSITES

Psychology Today: "The History and Psychology of Warrior Women"
www.psychologytoday.com/blog/whats-in-name/201508/the-history-and-psychology-warrior-women

This article examines how different cultures and historical periods have thought about and treated warrior women.

Women's History Month

womenshistorymonth.wordpress.com/resources/ women-and-series/women-and-war/female-warriors
For Women's History Month, this site offers a comprehensive list of women warriors who lived and fought during the Middle Ages.

Women Warriors

upfront.scholastic.com/issues/12_14_15/ women-warriors
A Scholastic/*New York Times* collaboration that provides students with articles about important current events, such as female soldiers graduating from Rangers school.

Women Warriors from 3500BC to the 20th Century

www.lothene.org/women/women.html
This website features an extensive list of all known women warriors in historical records from the birth of civilization until the twentieth century.

INDEX